Palewell Pr

Rented

Poems on prostitution and dependency

Sue Johns

Prostitution is not just a service industry, mopping up the overflow of male demand, which always exceeds female supply. Prostitution testifies to the amoral power struggle of sex, which religion has never been able to stop. Prostitutes, pornographers, and their patrons are marauders in the forest of archaic night.

Camille Paglia

Rented

Poems on prostitution and dependency

Rented – Poems on prostitution and dependency

First edition 2018 from Palewell Press www.palewellpress.co.uk

ISBN 978-1-911587-08-8

The cover design is Copyright © 2018 Camilla Reeve
The photos on the front and back cover are Copyright © 2018 Eugene Homewood

A CIP catalogue record for this title is available from the British Library.

Dedication

Dedicated to Patric, Agnes and Katy for their poetic support
and to the wonderful Eugene for life support.

Acknowledgments

'The Goose the Ghost and the Man' appeared in *Trespass* magazine, 2012.

'Watching Promise' was published as a members' prize poem in *Poetry News* 2017.

'Before the Pussy Riots', 'Remembering Mrs Lot' and 'Instructions for a Summer Wedding' all appeared in *Loose Muse* anthologies by *Morgan's Eye Press* 2012-2014. 'God Said' appeared in *Prole* magazine 2017.

'The Goose the Ghost and the Man' and 'The Dancer's Choice' were also published, by artist Lorraine Clarke, as part of an exhibition in 2014.

Contents

The Goose the Ghost and the Man

The Clink was my manor where I still reside with the whores
(The Winchester Geese), the paupers, the dispossessed.
In the still of a 21st century Sunday to the rattling of trains,
in the shadow of The Shard, through the countless
skulls and syphilitic bones, it is as goose I rise.

Not a bird fattened in the cloisters destined
for a Christmas plate, I am heroin chic,
super model thin as I slip through *The Red Gates*.
I caress its ribbons, poems, its tiny bears, a shrine
to the 'working girls' homespun and trafficked.

From my sisters of the past to those
who trade on the pavements of London,
Birmingham, Nottingham. Snuffed out
like the candles nestling in the weeds they
will burn again as the stones are turned to beating organs.

I honk and glide over the rooftops, the narrow
streets no longer running with stinking waste,
over the Bishop's ruins whose coffers
held the rent from the lodgings
where I spread my legs.

Over the market where I sold myself
at Southwark Fair. The wharfs that knew
mob rule, that rocked to music
and pleasures of the flesh, now
sterile boxes to seal the wealthy off.

Hissing over the singing Thames
to the seats of government, law, and finance -
the old haunts of the father I never knew.
I seek a certain type of gentleman.
I enter the safe sleep of lawyer, judge, stockbroker, priest.

In dreams they wrestle me in my room
at *The Anchor*, their portly bodies
enfolded in my wings. With a scratching in their groins
they awake perspiring on feather pillows
beside their cold and tidy wives,

dress to face an innocent morning, soap
me from their shiny skins. In hangman tight
ties, mildly harassed by the half-digested grass
upon their stairs they pause in doorways,
prepare to stride their importance into the light.

Before I launch, take flight to *Crossbones*,
their feet embed themselves in my excrement,
with a final twist of my elegant white neck
I rip through expensive shoe leather
and peck at their adulterous heels.

*Crossbones Cemetery is the sight of a medieval burial ground in
Southwark, London. Originally created for prostitutes known as The
Winchester Geese, after The Bishop of Winchester whose title permitted
prostitution on the South bank, for 400 years, in return for rent from
the brothels.*

2

Floralia

Is this the day of my honorable death?
The beasts are slain and now
the arena heralds man to slaughter man.
Must melancholy stain this tainted liberty?
Slave sisters, this is your time.

Leave your stone-cold beds in the fornices,
flesh and fluidity are the weapons you deploy.
The wind has swept the blossoms from the hillside,
the violets lie crushed by frozen rain.

Revive each rose upon the cheeks of an emperor,
bare your breasts for Flora and the mob,
let coloured cloth unwrap your nakedness. Go!
Sex the buds that will rupture sod –
the gods are the exponents of your wantonness.

Stir wombs under a shower of garbanzo,
rebirth, as I allow *The Circus* to do its worst.
Dance! Fornicate!
And may the frenzy you create ensure the bay
stays evergreen, to deck each favoured crown.

*Floralia was an ancient, Roman festival held in honour of the goddess
Flora. Prostitutes led most of the celebrations.*

Stag

The groom gets a rough crossing
in a shirt bearing **Stevies Stag** –
no apostrophe. A swaying
of medieval alleyways awash with neon.

With the last Heineken barely
punching the gut and the briefest glimpse
of the wares in a reddened window
he gets man-handled through a door
for an *early wedding present*.

Teodora *Not your real name.*
Yes my real name, after the saint.
Her body is blasphemy, her beauty
breaks the dawn over De Wallen
as the first trams ring out from Damrak
resounding like a Sunday morning.

As wedding heels are worn-in
hard, pink shellac taps out the final list.
Over prosecco a brood of hens
lay their plans of lace and cake.

for the over-fed lamb who will be
already bound as he waits at the altar.
His shoes, as grubby as ternate futures
and a trousseau of euros in a bedroom drawer.

Rented

That kiss was not the debutante's kiss
bought at De Beers
then deposited in the 'country pile.'

That kiss was certainly not the girl's kiss
purchased with ponies and funds in trust.

That kiss was not the kiss
in the back of the Daimler
that never was a kiss
but something more urgent
exchanged for a single note.

That kiss, one of many kisses
you will deliver in this stuccoed hallway,
was the 'boyfriend experience.'
Your manly hands enfolding his face,
your tongue at the back of his throat.
Such a kiss my dear, can only be rented.

A Friend of Promise

She was interrupting the stacking of Tampax,
waiting to receive her little cup of Meth
with one hand holding 'trackies' around
her skinny, white hips.
Ola and I exchanged raised brows.
I remember that, but not exactly when it was
that I decided to steal her. Or why
her in particular. Was it because she lived
across The Square? Or because she was
much younger than us other 'working ladies'?

But not too young to go 'doctor shopping', though.
She'd just traded one addiction
for another. I prayed over her
and on the third day of her sweaty sentence
she took a little jollof rice and soup
but I knew, when she ate my chicken stew,
the girl was clean.

'Clean enough to visit home' she said
'Come with me to The Chilterns,
fields and hills' she said.

She didn't need to explain why we didn't make it.
I heard it all on speaker-phone, how
she wouldn't bring drugs into their house,
and no niggers either
so we are to stay with her aunt in Southampton.
I asked if we'd still get fields and hills.
She said 'Promise, we will' and even better
she said 'We'll have the sea,
we'll have real fish and chips
and we'll have sailors.'

Watching Promise...

across The Square,
from under the tabby nets,
it seems a client has left her a gift.
My guess is a filthy finger nail
got married to her oily hip
and fathered some pus just out of reach
because she's using some dirty dance-moves
to squeeze it.

Promise knows this isn't like the hand-jobs
we give, off the kerb, ending in a heavy spurt.
This is a wound that'll spread
and come back weeping across an angry border.
It reminds me of those new girls,
when they stray into a foreign postcode.

Promise needs to put on the slippers
that make her look free again
(though she's formidable in heels)
and pay a visit to the prissy chemist

who will be relieved (not,) to be asked
for 'Morning Afters' or a cream for 'crabs',
though she'll still dispense that look
she reserves for an entire continent
watching Promise, bounce her box-braids
out of there with a crash
and the door-bell pinging.

This is our healing-time.
My friend rubs antiseptic
into the wet of her back-fat as The Square
takes a communal draw to the lungs,
watching Promise unlock her milky windows
to lie with her legs wide open
and let in some air.

Words that Promise Knows

WANTON:
A brazen *ashewo*,
who did not go home
to 'lay out' her mother.

WON'T:
The oath,
the pledge of disallowing,
the things she *no go do.*

FAITH:
Her allegiance to Jesus,
her belief *that betta don come.*

FACE:
No dorti slap,
her pan cake,
her beautiful gap-tooth smile.

PASSPORT:
Corner, corner,
a visa,
a key,
her safe conduct.

PASS OUT:
When she get *shayo*
and bury her pain.

CAN'T:
All of the impossible,
the bodi no bi firewood.

CUNT:
Or *kpekus.*
No matter the word -
they *go do am* again and again.

WANT:
She want *God go butter her bread*
and no more men
erect as headstones.

Before the Pussy Riots

1.

The brightly balaclava'd
ventured, where intrigue capered
amongst the bells and incense.
Unorthodox then
for punks
to dance and pray
to Virgin saints.
When can their glory fade?
Oh what a charge they made
Those girls, sentenced to sew
the warp of unease
only discarding
the weft of corruption
to queue for gulag fare
in lines as crisp
as Stalinist snow.

2.

To be violated was as criminal
as it was to love for
the believing women,
who draw their outer clothes
around them,
that they would be recognised
and not molested.
Freedom was claimed
in dreams, behind bars
and beneath burkhas
as their learned sisters
took to the skies
with the speed of flying acid -
their pages bullet-ridden,
their faces a curse upon
the naming of schools.

3.

It was written that
the nature of women
was to seduce men.
But the sound was red
as a naked girl hit the dust.
When her honour soaked the ground,
in a continent of coloured silk,
there was none to cover her.
The Preserver and
The Conqueror of Ignorance
were as any other idols -
bedecked with flowers,
being offered a light lunch
while Eve was teased.
Justice was measured in media coverage
as a dowry purse was counted
and a husband reached
for kerosene and matches.

Alfred, Lord Tennyson (The Charge of the Light Brigade)

The Quran 24.31

Manusmriti 2.213

14

God said...

that I am stranger than the honey on my lips.
My mouth is as smooth as oil -
easing me, along, to a bitter end.
These stilettos are bound for hell.

I say 'Couldn't your son wash his own feet?'
'Don't bring my hair into it
I'm dry-eyed and my perfume stays
right behind my ears.'

My attic brings salvation to many men
and my walls don't even crack.
This town isn't Jericho, baby -
I can worship the moon if I wish.

There is no faith to save me
I will not go in peace.

Remembering Mrs Lot

But his wife looked from behind him, and she became a pillar of salt.
Genesis 19:26
Come, let us make our father drink wine, and we will lie with him, that we may preserve the seed of our father. **Genesis 19:32**

You always looked over your shoulder –
checking my movements.
On our ungodly streets you turned
to the sounds of sodomy and sucking

so we silently closed our doors
and conceived our daughters, shrouded,
in the dark. They grew with a passion
alien to their begetting and strode before us

from our city in flames. It was then
that I whispered "Do you not wish
to see how all that irks you burns?"
You could not resist, and I laughed

at your pale pillar- the art of our maker
without mercy. I laugh as our offspring
ply me with wine - I have been drinking
their beauty for years.

And I take them, our angels,
held by the hair they will not turn
just writhe and work themselves a lineage
as I lick their bodies free of salt.

16